Our Story

*"When all seemed HOPELESS,
God came through
and gave us HOPE and a FUTURE!"*

Hennie Schoeman

Inks and Bindings
888-290-5218
www.inksandbindings.com
orders@inksandbindings.com

Contents

THIS IS

Our Story

Edma and Hennie Schoeman. (Picture 1973)
Written by Hennie Schoeman Revised 10/8/25

$\mathcal{I}$ was born in a small town named Klerksdorp in the Transvaal province, about a hundred miles South West of Johannesburg, South Africa on May 9th, 1952. My mother Cathy and father Abel(Boetie) Schoeman lived on the farm "Rheeboksfontein" about 10 miles outside the town. They both had committed their lives to God and we(my sister Kittie b.1953 and brother Anton b.1960) were privileged to grow up in a Christian home. They were active members of their church and served wherever possible.

Edma was born in Odendaalsrus, Orange Free State on August 9th 1953 to Mara and Eddie Hawley who also served the Lord and her and her siblings(Peter b. 1951, Suzette b. 1954 and Derek b. 1965) were raised in a similar home where God was served and they were also active members of their church.

After my father had a serious car accident on July 7th, 1961, which almost took his life, God led him to rent the farm and move to Johannesburg where, even though he had serious handicaps(he could not see well, walk or read well), God blessed him beyond measure and made him prosper in property investments and I remember him and mom taking me to a 14 acre piece of land in 1968 and saying that God wants us to buy this, build a house and dedicate it to the Lord. I will never forget the amazing sensation of the presence of the Lord when I first set foot on the property they named "Sela". When the new house was built and completed in December 1968, our family all went on our knees and dedicated the house to God. Soon after that we invited some friends to a prayer meeting on Saturday nights. word spread and before long we had 80 people in the lounge and dad asked everyone to take his seat(the ones who could) and we moved to the 1,600 sq ft garage. From then on we had services in the garage every Saturday night with people from many different denominations attending. Singing, sharing testimonies, praying for each other and on occasion we had some guest speakers.

Edma and I met in 1971 when Edma came with her church youth group to one of our meetings. Here's what happened: My father saw this beautiful young lady in our entrance hall and asked her what her name was. "Edma Hawley" she replied. To which he responded: "do you have a boyfriend?" Blushing, she answered "no sir" to which he replied "that's very good. Because I would like to have you as my daughter in law."

My father introduced us later that night and we courted for about 2 years before we got married in a fairy tale ceremony on May 5th, 1973. It was a God centered occasion and we made our promises to each other not knowing what the future had in store for us.

On the 7th day after the wedding, while still on honeymoon in the Malibu Hotel, Durban, Edma suffered a nervous breakdown. I had no idea what to do except pray. It was the sort of thing you read about and happens to others but which was not supposed to happen to you. I called my father and asked them to pray. We immediately went home where she was taken up in hospital. After examining Edma, the psychiatrist called me in and shared the scary diagnoses of manic schizophrenia with me. The prognosis: We could expect her to have break downs from time to time and with shorter intervals until she would probably be permanently confined to some institution. He said that they could nullify the marriage and that I could walk away from this very unfortunate situation, which according to him, was obviously a pre-existing condition and I was under no obligation to continue with the relationship. My answer was that I appreciated his opinion but that I remembered vividly a few weeks earlier making a promise, "until death do us part" and that I preferred to stick to my promise. "Remember I warned you and please don't ever consider having any children, because they would be at serious risk" the doctor told me. She was released after three weeks and a series of shock treatments, put on medication that would calm her down to the extent that she was not the same person we used to know. Dealing with depression became part of our daily lives.

My days would consist of going in to work at 7am and then coming back home, to our apartment in Windsor Park, at about 11am only to find Edma still in bed with no intention of getting up. I would then typically sit with her and give her all the reasons she had for getting up that I could think of. She had convinced herself that she had messed up my life and that there was not much point in living. Every time this happened, I realized that I needed to depend on the Holy Spirit to guide my words more than ever. Invariably, after spending an hour, or so, encouraging her and feeding her with every good reason to continue and not to give up, she would drag herself out of bed, get up and do her household chores of washing, cleaning and preparing dinner.

During this time, I learned to lean on God, and I got to know Him so much better than ever. I believed He would help us through whatever was to come, although I had no idea what that meant and what it would require of me. In the early part of 1974 Edma had a second break down and was hospitalized for six weeks, including another series of shock treatments, before being released again with strong medication.

In August of 1974, she fell pregnant with our first born and although she was distraught at first,(she cried for two weeks)an amazing transformation took place soon after. She became the perfect wife and mother to be. The gynecologist even commented on what a star patient she was. All medication was immediately reduced to levels that would not have a negative effect on our baby. Through the pregnancy we prayed asking God to prepare the perfect soul mate for our baby, we did not know that He had started that process in a different country already.

We were warned that the birth could trigger another break down and should be aware of the possibility. The morning of the birth, April 21st, 1975, we went in to the Park Lane Clinic in Johannesburg and I stayed with Edma all the time, while monitoring her every emotion. I remember her at one point, jumping off the bed and walking(almost running) in circles. She must have read my mind because she looked at me and said: "don't worry Hennie, I am not going mad, it's just very painful" I was immediately set at ease. We prayed together and trusted God to help her through the experience. She later gave a normal birth to Abel, our son, and she held up wonderfully through the whole process. She even posed for some pictures immediately afterward with our new baby boy. We thanked God for the special gift He had entrusted us with and promised to raise him in His ways.

Although she went back into a "gray" area of depression and zombi like condition, shortly after Abel's birth, she fell pregnant again when he was about nine months old. Then a miracle happened for the second time. She came back to normal while expecting our next baby. The time flew by and before we knew it, the time had come and Hendrik lll (she decided to name him after me-I was so honored) was born without complications.

At the time I had been working for a Christian ministry and had no medical insurance. The preacher, Thinus Trichaardt, felt he wanted to help us with the costs and took up an offering then handed me a check for the amount collected. It so happened to be the exact amount of the account we received from the doctor and the hospital. I was again overwhelmed with God's faithfulness.

When she was up to the task, Edma was the best mother the boys could wish for but her condition fluctuated and for me, it was a constant and conscious effort to help her with her emotional ups and downs while she was again on heavy medication to help keep her condition stabilized. We had since(when Abel was 7months old) moved to a condo in Berario, a suburb of Johannesburg, where we joined a church(AFM Johannesburg North) close to us, where we served and raised our children "under the pews in the second row". I served on the board and became youth leader while Edma supported me and we enjoyed a few relatively uncomplicated years.

Abel was five and Hennie four when Edma took a turn for the worst again. It was the most traumatic experience of my life when I was forced to physically "man handle" the love of my life, put her in the car and take her to see the psychiatrist at a mental hospital. Inside the doctor's office, I again had to restrain her...I will never forget how my tears flowed while man handling my best friend. She was admitted against her wishes(the equivalent of Baker Act)because her mood swings were totally uncontrollable. Amazingly, when the boys were in the room, she always calmed down and they were spared the agony of witnessing their mother's most extreme symptoms. The symptoms were so bad that she had to be locked up in the "padded cell" for fear of her causing injury to herself or others. She would receive a series of electric brain shocks during her three month stay.

While in hospital, I would visit her regularly and also brought the boys with me when she started stabilizing after the first two months. My visits were very cool and calculated, with a nurse never far away. We would meet in the lounge, where I would attempt to make conversation as best I could. Most of the time she would just stare at me and whisper her responses which I sometimes could understand. She loved apples and I would regularly bring her one to eat while we visited. On one occasion she took the apple, stared at it, slowly squashed it in her hand and with a blood curdling scream, threw it on the ground in a pulp. That was the end of our visit and the nurse took her back to her room.

On a few other occasions, she would start recognizing me and then she wouldn't let me leave. I would then have to tell her that I would be back soon and I would leave by a side door while she stayed and waited for me to return. I remember vividly how I would sneak up to the window of the lounge from the outside and watch her being led back to her room by the nurse. Those were times that I broke up in a million little pieces. Many nights I cried until there were just no more tears. No one could understand what we were going through. Not her parents nor mine, although they were extremely supportive, although they loved us both very much. Only God knew and I got to know Him better than ever during those troubled times.

By now I was working for another company and many nights, on my way back from the hospital, I would stop at my employer's office when I noticed his lights were still on. Andre Roeland was a real friend and would encourage me to keep the faith and not give up. He has since gone to be with The Lord but those times in his office I will treasure as long as I live. When Andre Crouch wrote the song "Through it All" during the sixties, I don't think he had the slightest idea of how the words of that song would support me through my ordeal. Through it all, I indeed learned to trust in Jesus and to trust in God.

After three months in hospital, the progress ended and with Edma's condition hanging in a very uncertain place, I decided to take it upon myself to, against doctor's wishes, sign her out and take her home.

At home, we decided to meet with a very highly respected physician by the name of Dr Davis. He examined Edma and ordered blood work. Two weeks later we went to see him again to hear the results and his recommendations. He looked her into her eyes through his very thick glasses and said: "Mrs. Schoeman, you are physically in perfect condition and there is nothing you need. However, I would like to refer you to one of my students who is now a practicing psychiatrist." This he did and we later met Dr. Eben Oberholster. After hearing our history, he made some changes to her medication. She slowly came out of her zombi-like state and returned to more normal person. The lithium he had prescribed also benefited her condition and within 3 months she was back to being the girl I fell in love with. This was a real miracle and we were so very grateful to God. Shortly afterward, because she still had difficulty in getting up in the mornings, we considered the possibility of her taking a job for the simple reason to motivate her to start the day. We saw an ad in our local newspaper for a pharmacy assistant up the road. I called the owner, who happened to be a fellow church board member, to ask if he would give Edma the position. He agreed and sent over a few sets of uniforms. She started a few days later and soon became well loved by both customers and fellow workers.

One of the side effects of the lithium, which we were unaware of, was the slowing down of her metabolism with the result she picked up weight. Having weighed about 96 lbs. up to that point it was a real problem for her when she got to around 150lbs. In desperation she asked the pharmacist if he could give her something to help her lose weight. Without researching it, he gave her some diet pills which had the opposite effect to her antidepressant medication. Within 24 hours, things went drastically wrong. I received a phone call from her employer in early June 1981 to inform me that she was saying strange things and tearing up customer's checks and throwing them into the trash. I called Dr. Oberholster immediately and explained what had happened and also about the diet pills she had taken. After using a few bad words, upon hearing about the diet pills, he asked me to take Edma to the hospital where he practiced and said that he would call ahead to make arrangements.

I went to pick up Edma from the pharmacy. As I opened the car door for Her, for only the second time in my life, I heard the sweet voice of my Father God speak to me. This what He said: "Hennie! don't be afraid, this is the last time she will ever have a break down like this. She will NEVER be sick from this again!" When I was unsure of what I had just heard, He repeated the message . It was an amazing, almost indescribable experience and I had NO DOUBT that it was God's voice. My attitude changed immediately from being sad to almost being jubilant in the knowledge that we just had to do what we could and that God would do the rest.

At the hospital, she sank to a very deep low, having to go through shock treatment, strong medication, being locked up in her room, before she started to turn around and improve. It was six weeks before Dr Oberholster called to say I could come and fetch her. Excitedly I put the two boys in the car and drove to the hospital. Now, before we were married we started a habit of whistling to each other if we were in a large store and separated. We would then know where the other was and would be able to find each other.

As we walked down the long hospital hallway, about thirty feet from her room, I suddenly heard the beautiful sound of her whistling and tears of joy rolled down my face for I knew I had my wife and the boys had their mother back. This time "for keeps" and so it was. We went back home and within a few days she was back at work. When our boys were a little older, she started working half days so she could be with them after school. A new life for us as a family, had just begun. We joined Rhema Ministries and I became very involved with the music ministry from 1982 to 1993. This was a very important time in the life of our family. Both Abel and Hennie committed their lives to God and were water baptized during our time there. Edma finally resigned from her job at the pharmacy, just a few years before we immigrated to the United States and settled in Tampa, Florida in January, 1994.

We were warned that moving Edma so far away from her family, could trigger a relapse. However, she stayed calm and never again showed any alarming symptoms at all.

The two of us made a promise to each other about that time, that we would never again take one day for granted but that we would try to live each day in such a way that, if it would be our last, we would have no regrets at all. It was one of the wisest decisions we ever made.

We found a good church, Faith Outreach Center, where Abel, our oldest son, met Deborah Cunningham and got married in 2001. They have two beautiful daughters, Kaitlyn and Anna. Hennie, our younger son, got married in 2004. They too have been blessed with two wonderful children, Hendrik IV, and Charlotte. What a joy for Edma and myself to witness our children serving God, raising their children in the ways of the Lord, and making a difference wherever they are. We could not be more proud of our four grandchildren!

In 1999, I contracted a bacterial blood infection and was hospitalized for six days while Edma was so supportive and a pillar of pure strength.

In 2006, I had quadruple by-pass surgery and once again Edma was strong through it all. As I was being wheeled out of the theatre, a close friend of ours looked at my swollen face and wept bitterly while Edma was ever so calm. She asked Edma why she was so calm and this is what she answered: "I have a promise. The bible says that if you honor your father and mother you will be blessed with a long life. If anyone ever honored his parents, it was Hennie. So you see, I am not worried at all." My wife today is someone who has touched the lives of so many people who God sends across her path. She fills herself with the Word, uplifting, edifying literature, music and television programs. She actively decides what she watches, reads, or what she listens to. The result is that she is so full of good things that she invariably astounds me in the way she deals with crisis. Never even giving a hint of defeat but rather soaring over every circumstance with God given victory. Wow! To think I could have missed all this if I had made the wrong choice or decision right in the beginning of our marriage. Thank God for His mercy.

We are literally living out many of the dreams we had as young people. Our children and their families are all serving God. We have been blessed with the most precious family we could have ever dreamed of. Our prayers that we prayed over our babies, while they were still in the womb, were answered indeed.

Fast forward to 2013, Edma was diagnosed with Breast cancer. After receiving three opinions, she made the decision to go through with a double mastectomy. Her recovery was miraculous. Tests revealed that all the cancer and any affected cells were removed successfully. When she did not show any normal emotional concern during the process or thereafter, she was asked why she did not show any emotions(letting it out, allowing her to cry..) she quickly responded: "those first 8 years of my marriage were hell. This surgery and experience was nothing compared to that" she said smiling comfortably and beaming with confidence. I was amazed and rejoiced with her through it all.

The song by Andre Crouch says: "if I never had a problem, I'd never know that God could solve it and I wouldn't know what faith in

God could do" ."...through it all....(with the emphasis on Through), I've learned to trust in Jesus, I've learned to trust in God. Through it all, through it all, I've learnt to depend upon his Word."

On May 5th, 2023, we celebrated our 50th wedding anniversary and shared it with about 80 of our friends and family. Our marriage is indeed a MIRACLE!

I hope this personal story inspires you too to put your trust in an infallible God. What He has done for us, He can surely also do for you.

Because of Calvary,

Hennie Schoeman ll

YouTube Link for My Music: @hennie77777

Hennie & Edma on Table Mountain, Cape Town, South Africa

Hennie & Hendrik(my grandson)

The two of us on our Wedding Day.

Our family

Our sons: Abel & Hennie Jr

Our sons: Abel & Hennie Jr